CODE QUEST

INCA GOLD

Written by Anita Croy

Illustrated by Mick Posen

KINGFISHER
LONDON & NEW YORK

Copyright © Kingfisher 2011
Published in the United States by Kingfisher,
175 Fifth Ave., New York, NY 10010
Kingfisher is an imprint of Macmillan Children's Books, London.
All rights reserved.

Distributed in the U.S. and Canada by Macmillan,
175 Fifth Ave., New York, NY 10010

Library of Congress Cataloging-in-Publication data
has been applied for.

Created for Kingfisher by Brown Bear Books Ltd.
Original concept: Jo Connor
Narrative concept: Simon Holland

ISBN 978-0-7534-6729-9

Kingfisher books are available for special promotions and
premiums. For details contact: Special Markets Department,
Macmillan, 175 Fifth Ave., New York, NY 10010.

For more information, please visit www.kingfisherbooks.com

Printed in China
1 3 5 7 9 8 6 4 2
1TR/0711/LFG/UNTD/200MA

4 MEET JULIETTA
How to use this book

6 PERUVIAN GOLD
Step into the past

8 AT THE MARKET
Follow the story

10 THE CORN CODE
Solve the codes

12 LINES IN THE DESERT
Follow the story

14 MYSTERIOUS LINES
Solve the codes

16 IN THE LOWLANDS
Step into the past

18 THE ICE MAIDEN
Follow the story

CONTENTS

 **20** KNOTTY PROBLEM
Solve the codes

 22 THE ANCIENT CAPITAL
Follow the story

24 GOLDEN LLAMA
Solve the codes

 26 CHILD SACRIFICE
Step into the past

 28 WEALTHY EMPIRE
Step into the past

 30 ON THE INCA TRAIL
Follow the story

32 CHALK MESSAGE
Solve the codes

 34 SACRED VALLEY
Step into the past

 36 SECRET CITY
Follow the story

 38 A NEW MESSAGE
Solve the codes

 40 MACHU PICCHU
Step into the past

 42 INTO THE MOUNTAINS
Follow the story

44 REVEALED!
Solve the codes

46 INDEX
Where to find things

48 THE SOLUTIONS
Check your answers

I'm Julietta. I'm a student in Lima, the capital of Peru. Get ready. You are going to help me solve a mystery that will take us back to Peru's past and the remarkable empire of the Inca.

MEET JULIETTA

Who is the mysterious figure who leads the way?

Dear Code Breakers,

I love finding out about the Inca who used to live in Peru. I was reading a great book about them, which my dad had found for me, when my mom sent me to the market. I did not want to leave my book, but my trip turned into an adventure that took me all over the country. It led me high into the mountains—and back into the past. Along the way, I had to break lots of coded messages. Now you will have a chance to solve them yourself in this book. Good luck!

At the end of my journey, I found out something very special. For that, I had to thank my new friend Arturo . . . and our mysterious guide.

Here is your challenge: read my story and look at all the clues and evidence I found. Can you break the different codes, read the ancient pieces of writing, and solve the mystery along with me?

Inca god stamped on gold plate

Look out for the evidence in each exciting scene.

Even the smallest detail could reveal a vital clue.

HOW TO USE THIS BOOK

As you read the book, you will see exciting scenes from my adventure. These are followed by "code breaker" pages, in which I set out all of the clues for you to study. Evidence panels show you the key codes in the story and tell you what you need to do to crack them. It is a good idea to make sure you have your code wheel nearby!

SECRET SYMBOLS

SECRET SYMBOLS

These symbols (above) are not as scary as they look. As we go along, I will give you hints to help you translate them into English.

MISSING WORDS

As you decode the symbols, you may need to fill in verbs (action words) and other words to make sense of them. Use your common sense!

THE CHARTS

Look out for foldout charts that summarize the information you need to break the codes.

CODE BREAKER

SYMBOLS IN THIS BOOK
The Inca had no written language. This book uses a code to create puzzles and challenges for you to solve—but although they are based on Inca designs, the symbols are made up. The names given to them (below) are also made up. Like some ancient languages, this 'Inca' language uses symbols to stand for words rather than for individual letters. You should keep in mind as you solve the puzzles that some verbs (doing or action words) and conjunctions (linking words) will need to be added to make a complete sentence.

CODE WHEEL CLUE
Throughout the book, you will need to piece together broken symbols, identify them using this chart, and then set your code wheel. The wheel will then help you translate the clues in the story.

It may help if you trace the broken symbols onto paper, cut them out, and fit them together that way.

SLOPE	PYRAMID	ZIPPER	TABLE
DIAMOND	TRIANGLE	CASTLE	MAZE
FOUR XXXX	SNAKES	CROSS	ZIGZAGS	BUTTONS	ENVELOPE
SNAKE SQUARE	BACKWARD SLOPE	ARROWHEADS	VILLAGE	PILLARS	SCROLL

The charts show you the ancient symbols and the words or phrases that match up with them.

INCA CODES

The Inca had no system of writing. The codes on these pages have been created specifically for this book and are completely fictional.

HOW TO SET YOUR CODE WHEEL

Your code wheel has two parts: an outer ring of symbols and an inner ring with words and phrases in the modern English alphabet.

Step 1. On the code-breaker pages, you will be asked to put together four broken pieces to form a complete symbol from the outer ring of the code wheel.

Step 2. Turn the inner ring of the wheel so that the arrow points to the symbol you have discovered.

Step 3. With the rings in the same position, you can now read the meaning for each symbol in a particular code.

SOLUTIONS

If you get stuck on a code, take a look at page 48, where all of the answers are given and explained.

But no cheating! The harder you try to solve the codes yourself, the better you will get.

Peru was home to many ancient civilizations. The most famous are the Inca, whose empire grew far beyond Peru's modern borders. But at its peak their powerful empire lasted only 100 years.

PERUVIAN GOLD

TREASURES
Ancient Peruvians left many remarkable traces: buildings, roads, textiles, pottery—and gold . . . lots of gold.

TWO LANDSCAPES
The Andes Mountains split Peru in two, with jungle on the eastern, inland side and desert on the western, coastal side. Early civilizations settled by the coast, but the Inca lived in the mountains.

The Inca built more than 25,000 mi. (40,000km) of roads to link their empire. The roads zigzagged up mountainsides.

ECUADOR

• Chan Chan

PACIFIC OCEAN

Andes

Andes

PERÚ

• Lima

Machu Picchu

Sacred Valley • •
Cusco

• Paracas

• Nazca

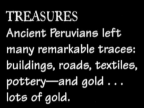

The Andes rise like a wall between the dry coast and the rainforest farther inland.

The Inca capital of Cusco (also spelled Cuzco) lay in the heart of the mountains.

SACRED ANIMALS

The Inca revered the jaguar of the forests and the puma (cougars) that lived in the mountains. The cats often featured in Inca art. The Inca capital of Cusco was laid out in the shape of a crouching puma.

Cup in the shape of a jaguar

MOUNTAIN STEPS

The Inca did not have much flat land, but that did not worry them. They made the most of mountain slopes by shaping them into narrow, flat terraces (steps in the land) where they could grow crops.

KEY CROPS

The Inca ate little meat. Their main foods were potatoes and corn—but they might find today's yellow corn a little boring. Inca corn was all kinds of colors, including blue. It was not only used for food; the Inca also turned it into a beer known as *chicha*.

A long, long time before freezers were invented, the Inca learned how to freeze-dry potatoes naturally so that they could be stored and eaten all year long.

GREAT ACHIEVEMENTS

The Inca and the other early peoples of Peru created highly successful civilizations. We can still see traces of some of their achievements today. Others we can read about in the accounts of the Spanish, who overthrew the Inca Empire in 1532.

They were great craftspeople who made fantastic masks and carvings out of gold. Gold was so valuable that the Inca used it to make offerings to their gods.

They made colorful textiles from wool that they wove into complex patterns. Some cloth patterns are so detailed that experts wonder if they might contain some kind of secret code.

They were expert builders who used huge stones to construct massive temples and fortresses. The stones fit together so well that the walls have survived many earthquakes—even though the Inca did not use any cement.

They were skilled farmers. They used terraces and irrigation, or water channels, to grow crops to feed their people. They stored food to use in times of drought, when there was very little rain.

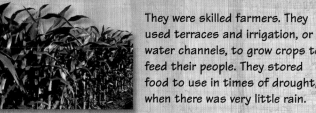

Although the Inca did not have a form of writing, they kept records by using bundles of knotted strings, known as *quipus*—but no one knows what the quipus meant!

AT THE MARKET

I usually like going to the market, but today I was in a hurry
to get back to the book my dad had given me. It had me
wondering: could we possibly be descended from the Inca?

There were lots of people waiting at the stall where
I normally buy vegetables, but I didn't want to wait.
The stall nearby had no one at it. It would be much quicker.
"I've never noticed this one before," I thought as I bought
corn for supper. I did not pay much attention to the stall
worker. His hat hid his face, but I guessed from his clothes
that he had brought his vegetables down from the mountains.

I rushed off so quickly that I didn't see the hole in the road.
Suddenly, I tripped and the food went flying. I picked
it all up—but one corncob looked very different from the
others. It was dark and shiny. When I picked it up, it felt
cool and hard. It was really heavy. Gold! Solid gold!

There had been some mistake. I wondered what to do—
but the answer was clear. The golden corn wasn't mine.
I had to give it back to the man at the market.

When I got back to the market, there was no sign of the man.
I looked for clues about where he might have gone.
I wanted to give him his golden corn back.

THE CORN CODE

The boxes on the man's stall had labels on them. One was very smudged.

I looked around for clues. There was some paper with writing on it and a train ticket. I wondered if the golden corn itself might be able to tell me anything.

CODE TWO: THE TICKET CODE

I wondered if the numbers on the ticket meant something. Perhaps number 1 stood for A, 2 for B, and so on. Can you figure out two place names? But beware! Some pairs of numbers may make one letter—13 might mean AC or it might mean M, the 13th letter of the alphabet.

129131
TO
1412631

CODE ONE: THE LABEL
The label had become wet and smudged so that the words were all blended together. Can you figure out what it says?

ittakestwoears
tolearnthesecret
ofthegoldencorn

A ticket had fallen onto the floor. It must have been in the bag with the golden corn.

SET YOUR CODE WHEEL

Put these pieces together to find out how to set the wheel for this code.

It was only when I looked closely at the corn that I saw that it had symbols stamped on it.

CODE THREE: THE CORN CODE

There were four symbols on the golden corn. They looked like patterns I'd seen on ancient textiles or in ancient artwork.

Whatever the message says, it must be very short. Perhaps it says something about who owned the golden corn or where it came from. How old was it? I had a feeling the corn might be about to send me on an adventure.

Can you use the code breaker under the flap (right) to set your code wheel and figure out what the message says?

CODE BREAKER

LINES IN THE DESERT

I used the ticket to catch the train to Nazca. There, I headed to the market. There was no sign of the mysterious stall worker. Then I thought I saw him heading down an alley. I followed, but when I reached the alley, he was turning another corner. I ran harder.

"Look out!" I crashed straight into a young man. "Where did he go?" I said. "Who? I'm the only person here." I looked around. We were on the edge of town. The desert stretched on for miles. Nearby was a small hole. "That's my dig," the man explained. "My name's Arturo. I'm an archaeologist. I'm investigating the Nazca lines." He showed me a drawing of some shapes from the lines.

I had an idea. I showed him the corncob. "Do you recognize this? Is it from Nazca?" "No," he said. "But I have seen something similar. It was wrapped in cloth like this." The man pointed to some beautiful material he had found. "This is what people used to wrap dead bodies in. Some experts think the patterns might be a code. Perhaps they can give us some clues about your golden corn."

Arturo looked at the message on the corn. "There were codes everywhere in ancient Peru," he explained, frowning. "Like these patterns on the cloth. Even the Nazca lines might be a kind of code."

MYSTERIOUS LINES

Arturo had copied down some symbols from the desert. "But who could see them?" I asked. "They make sense only from the air." "We may never know," Arturo said, laughing. "Maybe the gods!"

The shapes were too big to make out in the desert, but they were clear in the drawing.

LONG-LASTING LINES
Arturo told me that the Nazca lines were formed by digging shallow trenches in the reddish desert, exposing the light-colored soil below. There is little wind, so the lines are well preserved.

CODE FOUR: GUESS THE SHAPES
These are all shapes drawn in the Nazca desert. Can you guess what archaeologists think they represent?

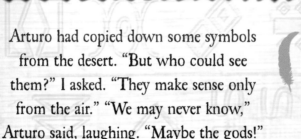

Clue: a big swimmer

Clue: you and me

Clue: swings in the trees

Clue: woof, woof!

Clue: bird of the Andes

Clue: chatty bird

CODE BREAKER

Ancient Peruvian peoples, such as the Paracas culture, were expert weavers. Their designs used squares with patterns inside. Some archaeologists think that these patterns might have contained messages—a little like wearing a T-shirt with words on it. Perhaps the patterns revealed where the wearer came from. It is impossible to know for sure. We have made up this code to show how it might have worked.

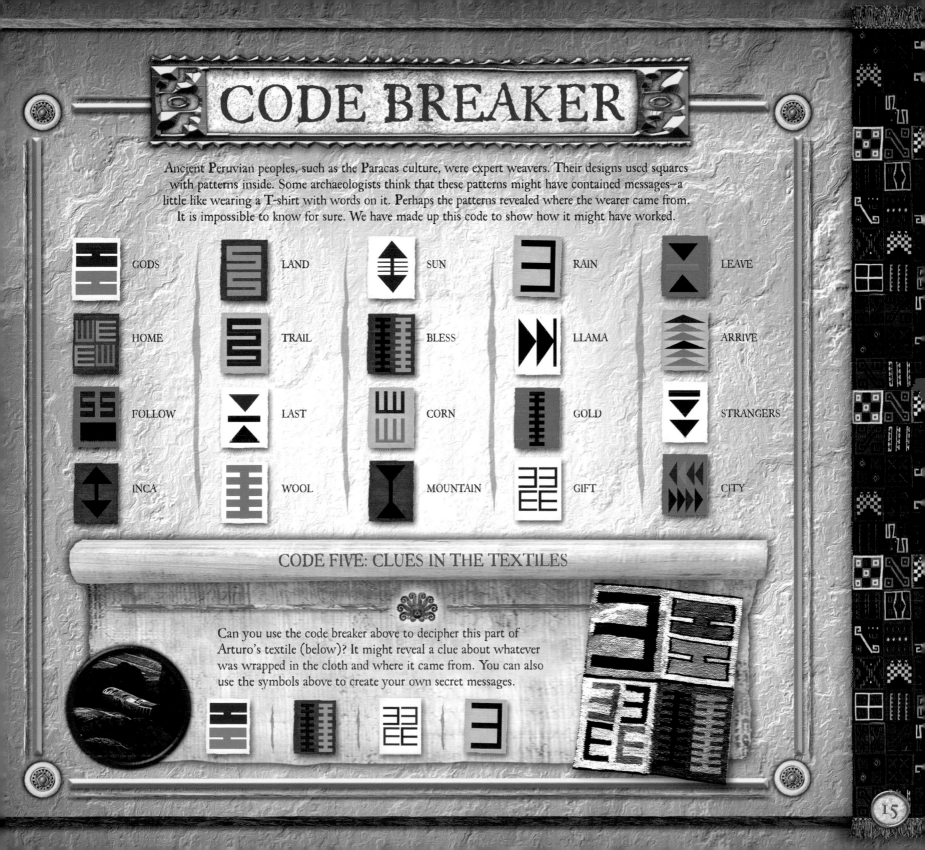

GODS

HOME

FOLLOW

INCA

LAND

TRAIL

LAST

WOOL

SUN

BLESS

CORN

MOUNTAIN

RAIN

LLAMA

GOLD

GIFT

LEAVE

ARRIVE

STRANGERS

CITY

CODE FIVE: CLUES IN THE TEXTILES

Can you use the code breaker above to decipher this part of Arturo's textile (below)? It might reveal a clue about whatever was wrapped in the cloth and where it came from. You can also use the symbols above to create your own secret messages.

The Inca were one of many peoples who lived in **Peru**. Civilizations such as the **Chimú**, the **Moche**, and the **Paracas** once lived near the coast. After centuries, the desert is slowly giving up their secrets.

IN THE LOWLANDS

CITY OF BRICK

The largest city of ancient Peru, Chan Chan, was built in about A.D. 900 by the Chimú. The imperial capital was home to walled palace compounds, with temples and storehouses. Its adobe (sun-dried mud) walls have many geometric patterns and bird motifs.

WOVEN INTO HISTORY

From around 500 B.C., the Paracas people of southern Peru wrapped their dead in layers of colorful feathers and cloth. The bright cloth wrapped around the mummies was woven with images of priests, animals, and warriors. The textiles have been preserved by the dry climate of the desert. The woven images reveal that the Paracas practiced human sacrifice to keep the gods happy.

On the floor of the Nazca desert near the coast of central Peru are many lines hundreds of feet long that make dozens of different shapes. One looks like a monkey, another a spider, and another like a killer whale. The Nazca people created the lines around A.D. 500.

Archaeologists still puzzle over what the lines were for. Some of them can be seen clearly only from the air. They might have been religious symbols. Or perhaps they were a kind of calendar tracing the movement of the stars.

Llamas were the main beasts of burden in the river valleys where the Moche lived.

MUMMIES

The Nazca buried their dead in brick vaults beneath the desert sands—where they are still often preserved. They dressed the body in his or her best clothes and provided valuable gifts for the gods.

1 Ornamental beads

2 Decorative bracelets

3 Textiles of a higher quality were buried with the wealthiest people in society.

4 The dead were buried with their most valuable jewelry.

BRICKS AND POTS

The Moche lived in northern Peru from about 200 B.C. to A.D. 700. They used almost 200 million mud bricks to build temples to the sun and moon. Moche potters made vessels in the shape of people and animals, including this llama.

THE ICE MAIDEN

Arturo said that his colleague Henry might help decipher
the code on the golden corn. "Can we ask him?" I said.
"Yes," he said. "But we'll have to go up to the mountains."

We drove across the desert. The road climbed higher
and higher. Arturo said, "Did you know that Peru has
the highest archaeological sites in the world?"

When we found Henry and his team, they were examining
a pile of rags. Henry said, "Look. Isn't she beautiful?"
I saw with a shock that the bundle had a face. It was a child!

"Meet Conchita," said Henry. "She's been here for 600 years."
"But who left her here?" I asked.
"The Inca thought that gods lived in the mountains," said
Henry. "They left children as sacrifices. Look. That's why
she is wearing her best clothes."

"We found these with her." He pointed to a bundle of colored
strings with knots tied in them. "Those are the Inca way of
writing. Perhaps they were a message to the gods."

Arturo studied the bundle of strings with the girl mummy. "This is a quipu," he said. "The strings might tell us something about where Conchita came from or who left her here."

KNOTTY PROBLEM

"Conchita's quipu might have been a message for the gods," said Arturo.

Arturo explained that the Inca used the knotted strings as writing to keep records. Then I noticed familiar symbols on one of the pots near the girl's feet. I showed Arturo and Henry. They got quite excited. "Sacrifices were left with gifts for the gods," Arturo explained. "There might be another clue here about where Conchita came from."

Original Inca quipus still survive—but we don't know what they mean.

CODE SIX: CONCHITA'S HOME

To help you learn where Conchita came from, I've put the quipu strings in order. You can figure out what they spell by using the A-Z chart under the flap (right).

Almost all of the Inca names we know are of rulers, whose title was also "Inca."

CODE SEVEN: A ROYAL NAME

Arturo and Henry thought that some of the quipu strings might reveal the identity of the ruler who had sacrificed Conchita on the mountain. Again, you'll need to use the chart under the flap (right) to decode the emperor's name.

The symbols on the pot were like those on my golden corn. Use your code wheel to decode the message and learn where we have to head to next in our quest for the Inca gold.

The symbols looked like the ones on the corn. Arturo said, "This might be a message for us."

The Inca made quipus from the shaggy coat of the llama.

SET YOUR CODE WHEEL

To align the code wheel for the pottery code, put these pieces together to see which symbol the arrow should point to.

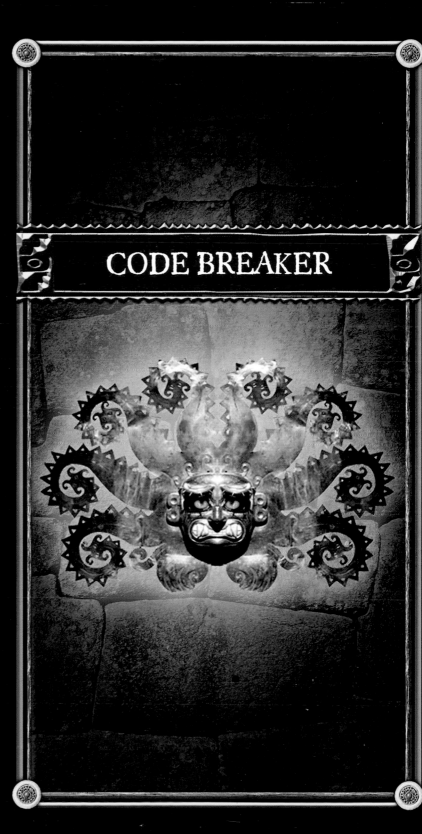

CODE BREAKER

THE ANCIENT CAPITAL

Henry thought that something as beautiful as the golden corn must have been made in the Inca's most important city. He suggested we head for Cusco.

As Arturo drove, I wondered what we might find. But nothing prepared me for the sight of Cusco sitting in a valley among the mountains. We made our way to the center.

"Look," Arturo said. Near a church was a display for tourists. It had a picture of a garden full of golden corncobs! The sign said that this was the Coricancha, an Inca temple to the sun.

While we were reading, Arturo felt a hand on his shoulder. "Hey!" he said. We spun around . . . and found ourselves face to face with an ancient Inca!

The man was wearing a yellow headdress and a short robe made of brown and orange cloth. He had a shawl draped over his shoulders. I saw that he was not alone.

He was one of eight men carrying a silver throne on their shoulders, four on each side. On the throne sat a woman wearing a headdress covered in golden rays.

The Inca whispered, "Study the sign. It will take you back to old Cusco." Then he was gone. I wondered what he meant. Then I saw Arturo studying the display.

GOLDEN LLAMA

The gold and silver garden showed just how vital the corn crops were to the Inca.

"Look at this painting," he said. "There's the garden of gold and silver corn."
I looked closely. "There's writing on that corn," I said.
Arturo took out a magnifying glass. "There! It's a code.
It's on the golden llama, too."

RITUAL RECREATED
Arturo explained that Cusco was a center for rituals dedicated to the sun. The parade we saw was of the Inca's descendants carrying on the same tradition.

CODE NINE: TEMPLE PRAYER

On one corncob, I could just make out two rows of symbols. Can you decode the message that the Inca left to their gods in the temple?

I made some notes about Cusco from the display.

The city was founded by Manco Cápac in the 1200s. Many stories are told about how Manco Cápac was the founder not just of the city but also of the entire Inca people. The Inca established the first parts of their empire in the area immediately around the city.

When the Spanish conquerors arrived in Cusco in 1533, they were astonished. One of them wrote about Cusco, "It is so beautiful and has such fine buildings that it would even be remarkable in Spain."

At the heart of the Inca city was the Coricancha. The temple was dedicated to the sun god, Inti. The building was covered with layers of gold that made it seem as if it shone. There were silver statues of gods in the streets.

The Spaniards made Cusco their capital. The old walls were so strong that they just built new buildings on top of the Inca foundations. The Coricancha became the site of a Spanish church.

The Inca fled . . . but where did they go?

CODE TEN: THE LLAMA CODE

I wrote down the symbols from the llama to make them easier to read, and I have set them out for you above. I hoped that they would give directions to somewhere. I was eager to find out the next destination on our journey. Where was the golden corn leading us? Use your code wheel to decipher this phrase and find out.

SMALL BUT SIGNIFICANT
Most golden llamas were tiny, but the llama's message might be the most important clue yet!

NO CEMENT!
Inca walls did not use cement. Instead, the Inca shaped stones to make them fit together. Some stones have up to 16 sides. They fit together so snugly that you cannot slide a piece of paper between them. This helped the ancient walls survive earthquakes that toppled newer buildings.

The llama was a very important animal in Inca life. It was so vital that it was included in Inca religion.

Arturo looked at me. "I bet I know where these clues will lead us," he said. "Cusco is the start of an amazing ancient path—the Inca Trail."

SET YOUR CODE WHEEL
Piece this symbol together and learn where to align the arrow on the wheel for both codes on these pages.

Walls in Cusco

CODE ELEVEN: WRITING ON THE WALL
There was a message written on a wall near the display. Fit the stones into the gaps to read what it said.

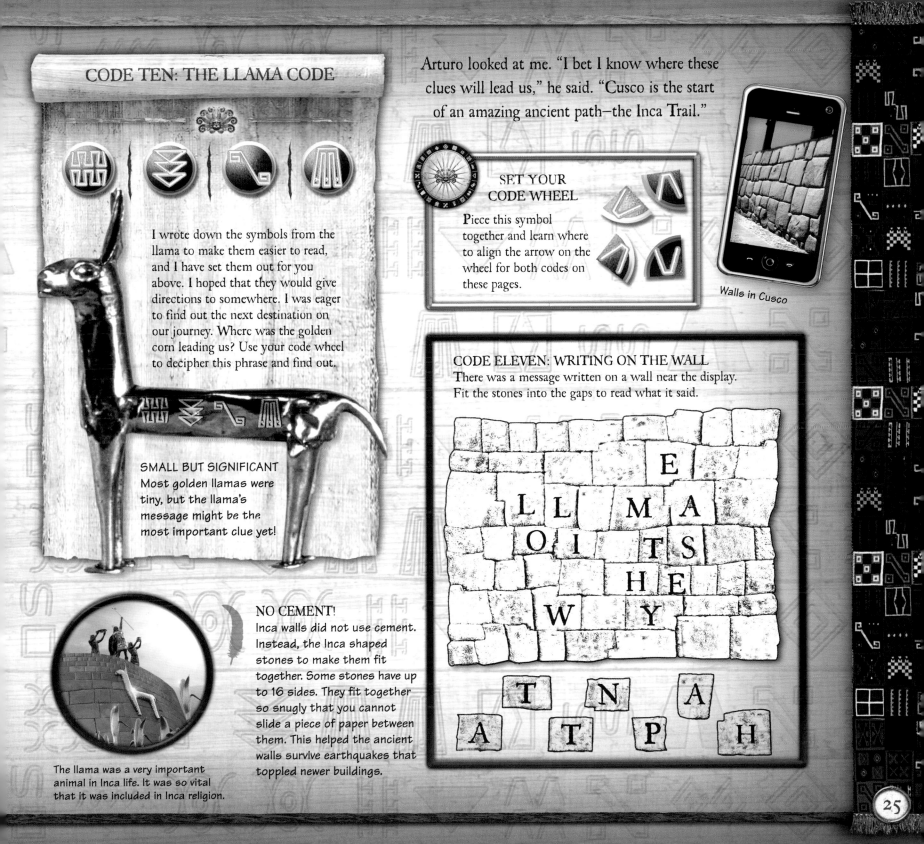

For the Inca, the most important duty was keeping the gods happy. They gave the gods precious gifts. The most precious was human blood . . . and the most highly prized was that of children.

CHILD SACRIFICE

Gold disk showing Inti

SACRED MOUNTAINS
The Inca may have believed that the peaks of the Andes were closest to the gods, especially the sun god, Inti. They led children in processions up the mountains—and sacrificed them there for the gods.

THE INCA GODS
The Inca believed that their rulers descended from Inti, the sun god, whose face was often shown as a gold disk (above). Another major god was Apu Illapu, the rain god who made the crops grow. Inti's sister and wife, Mama Kilya—the moon goddess—was usually shown as a silver face.

Carved stone face of a god

26

It was no wonder that the Inca's main god was Inti, the sun god. The Inca could see that the sun gave them light and kept them warm. Along with the rain, the sun made their crops grow.

The Inca believed that all of their emperors descended from Inti. They dedicated shrines to the god and made images of the sun out of gold. In the lost city of Machu Picchu, a sacred hitching post was used to keep ahold of the sun and stop it from escaping.

SUN CEREMONY

Every winter, the Inca marked the winter solstice—the shortest day of the year—with a festival held in Cusco in honor of Inti. The Inti Raymi, or Festival of the Sun, involved nine days of processions, dances, and animal sacrifices. Since 1944, the Inca's modern descendants have held a reconstruction of the festival in Cusco.

MOUNTAIN MUMMY

Preserved for centuries on mountaintops are the bodies of young Inca children. Tests on the frozen bodies revealed what they ate for their last meals. Some were killed by blows, others by being drugged. They wore clothes of beautiful textiles fastened with silver pins.

1 Well-preserved hair

2 Dyed colors are still bright

3 Legs bound in place with rope

27

Gold and silver made the Inca rich. The Inca did not even need to mine precious metals. They picked up nuggets of gold and silver from the ground and panned for gold in streams and rivers.

WEALTHY EMPIRE

Sacred puma made from gold

GOLD AND SILVER

When the Spaniards arrived in Cusco, they could not believe their eyes. Buildings dazzled in the sun because they were covered in gold. There was even a garden full of crops made from gold. The Inca called gold "the sweat of the sun" and silver "the tears of the moon." Gold was the symbol of Inti, the sun god, while silver represented Mama Kilya, the moon goddess.

Silver and gold shaped into elaborate jewelry

SACRED STREAMS

The streams of the Andes were rich in gold that could be washed from the gravel. The Inca treated the streams as sacred and prayed to their spirits. The production of gold and silver was controlled by the empire, which did not want too much of the metals to be mined.

Necklace of gold and precious stones

Gold and jewels hammered into attractive shapes

NATURAL WORLD

The crafts of the Inca, like those of other Andean peoples, celebrated the close connection between humans and the natural world. Animals were a constant theme in pottery and metalwork. The Inca thought that many animals were sacred, so animal decoration might have made everyday objects a bit more special.

A WEALTHY EMPIRE

The Inca did not use money. They exchanged labor and goods for what they needed. Everyone had to work for the empire as a form of taxation (known as *mita*), building roads or growing crops. Food was carefully stored by the empire, so no one went hungry when the harvest was poor.

Gold earrings decorated with turquoise stones

The Inca were expert craftspeople. They made beautiful objects, both for high-ranking people in society and to offer to the gods. Craftspeople made necklaces and bracelets out of gold and silver and decorated them with precious and semiprecious stones. They used bright parrot feathers to make headdresses that the Inca rulers wore during special ceremonies.

The Inca made clay pots that they painted with beautiful geometric designs. They also made their own clothes and blankets by weaving small squares of llama or alpaca wool and then joining them together.

Images of a winged, bird-headed god

ON THE INCA TRAIL

Arturo led the way as the path rose up the steep side of the valley. I wondered where it led. "The Inca thought that this whole valley was sacred," explained Arturo. "It was home to many of their most holy places."

The hillsides had been cut into what looked like giant steps. "The Inca dug these terraces to grow corn. They needed as much land as possible to grow enough corn to feed everyone."

Beyond the terraces lay some stone ruins. Arturo explained that they were ancient temples. We found a stone pillar that stood on a flat platform. Arturo said, "That's a hitching post. The Inca thought that if the sun was tied to the post, it couldn't get away."

I had the feeling that we were being watched— but when I looked around, I couldn't see anyone there. Something made me walk around to the far side of the hitching post. There was writing on it! I recognized the code. It was the same as the one on the golden corn!

Arturo rubbed at one of the characters on the hitching post. It smudged! "This is chalk," he said. "It's still fresh. Someone must have written this message recently. Very recently . . ."

CHALK MESSAGE

I still had the feeling that we were being watched, but I couldn't see any sign of anyone else. I tried to forget about it while I looked at the marks on the stone post. Why would someone write messages in an ancient Inca code?

CODE TWELVE: THE HITCHING POST

It seemed almost as if the chalk message had been left just for us. Perhaps someone wanted to tell us something. That made it even more important that we decoded it. Can you use your code wheel to see where the message told us to go?

In the Sacred Valley

I made some notes of what Arturo told me in case it helped explain the code.

There are temples to the sun, the moon, the rain, and the stars. The most important were dedicated to the sun.

The Inca believed that different gods controlled their world. They had to keep the gods happy.

The chalk was a little smudged—whoever had written the message had been in a hurry.

SET YOUR CODE WHEEL
The message should be clear if you turn your code wheel to point to the symbol shown in these four pieces. But remember that the code provides only the main words: you may have to fill in some gaps.

We continued walking. I glimpsed a flash of white far ahead on the path. It disappeared around a bend. When I saw it again, I was sure it was a white shirt. Was it the stall worker? But what would he be doing here?

"Look," said Arturo. "Someone's trying to tell us something."

CODE THIRTEEN: THE OLD SIGNPOST

Arturo was pointing to a signpost. The writing on it was old and worn, but it was clear that it wasn't just a simple place name. Some of the letters were smudged or missing, and it was hard to tell where words started or finished. I wrote down the letters that I could make out. Can you figure out the message?

lk/fr/a/
mssge/n/
th/cty/tht/
is/sacrd/to/
th/gds

TERRACES LIKE TARGETS
We passed a weird sight: the Inca had built some terraces that were completely circular. Can you guess why? No one knows the real answer, but Arturo said that some archaeologists think that the circles were like a laboratory for experimenting with plants. The Inca could test to see which crops grew best facing in different directions, for example.

LIVING LANGUAGE
The people who live in the Sacred Valley are modern descendants of the Inca. They still speak Quechua, the Inca language. About seven million people in South America speak Quechua today.

The terraces on the hills are still used by farmers. I like the idea that the people are still in touch with the past.

Beyond the Inca capital, Cusco, stretched the valley of the Urubamba River. Guarded by mountains, the Sacred Valley kept the secrets of the Inca for centuries.

SACRED VALLEY

HUMAN TRACES

Despite its remoteness, the valley bears many signs of human activity. High on its sides are temples and other structures. Terraces line the slopes. The valley floor was irrigated by waters diverted from the Urubamba for farming. At the valley's far end rose the peaks that were home to the sacred city of Machu Picchu.

Musicians entertained Inca builders and farmers.

The Inca built sites throughout the valley. The massive fortress of Sacsayhuamán (below), built in the shape of a puma, was an awe-inspiring stage for religious festivals. The ancient town of Pisac has terraces and towers that archaeologists believe may have been used as observatories to study the stars. It was the site of intensive irrigation. Deep in the valley, the fortress of Ollantaytambo was home to Manco Inca, one of the last Inca leaders, after Cusco fell to the Spaniards.

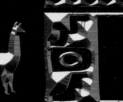

VALLEY OF THE GODS

The Inca worshiped huacas, which were natural sites or human-made features where the spirits of the gods lived. The valley of the Urubamba was full of huacas.

CAPITAL CITY

Cusco was built in a natural bowl surrounded by mountains. The wall builders did not use cement, but the huge stones fit together so well that they have survived many earthquakes.

IMPORTANT SITES IN THE SACRED VALLEY

- CUSCO—Inca capital
- Sacsayhuamán—fortress and ritual center
- Pisac—royal estate and agricultural terraces
- Ollantaytambo—royal estate
- Qoriwayrachina—mining city
- Machu Picchu—ceremonial city

INCA TIMELINE

c. 1100	The Inca rise to power in Cusco
c. 1190	Manco Cápac becomes the ruler of Cusco; Inca power begins to increase
c. 1390	Viracocha begins his rule of the Inca
1438	Pachacuti becomes emperor and begins wars of conquest over neighboring peoples
c. 1450	Machu Picchu is built
c. 1460	The Inca overthrow the Chimú
1471	Túpac Inca inherits the throne and extends the empire by warfare
1493	Empire reaches its largest extent
1528	Spaniards arrive in Peru
1532	Collapse of Inca Empire
1572	Death of Túpac Amaru, the last leader of the Inca people in Vilcabamba

This *aryballus*—a jar for carrying liquid—has typical Inca decoration using simple shapes.

Arturo caught up. "I was trying to tell you," he said. "This was no ordinary city. It was probably used only for ceremonies. The whole place is like one huge temple."

A NEW MESSAGE

We studied the message in the stone. The carvings looked very old. Perhaps they were Inca. "Look!" Arturo pointed. Beside the hitching post, someone had dropped a bundle of string. It was another quipu.

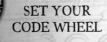

The code was carved into the base of the hitching post, which the Inca called Intihuatana.

SET YOUR CODE WHEEL

As usual, put together the symbol to find out where to align the arrow on the wheel to decode the message.

CODE FOURTEEN: HITCHING POST MESSAGE

The code in the stone was getting familiar now—but I noticed that the meanings of the symbols kept changing. I wondered what this message meant. Perhaps it was a message from the Inca to the sun that they worshiped at this spot. Can you use your code wheel and brains to figure out the message in the stone?

The buildings were used to store grain, not for housing people.

The city was full of terraces built into the mountainside.

The upper part of Machu Picchu (above) was a royal enclosure.

POPULAR SITE

Machu Picchu was crowded. No wonder! It's one of the most popular destinations on the planet. So why did no one else seem to notice the code carved in the stone? Perhaps it was because only we knew where to look—because the stall worker had led us there.

I wondered if Machu Picchu was the end of our journey. Then, high on a ridge, I caught sight of the stall worker's white shirt. He was walking into the mountains. "Come on." I grabbed Arturo. "Let's follow him."

CODE FIFTEEN: QUIPU DIRECTIONS

I felt that the quipu was meant for us. Perhaps it would tell us where to head next. Can you use the code breaker on page 21 to figure out our next destination?

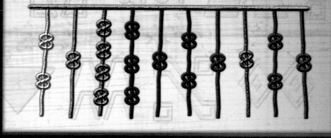

CODE SIXTEEN: TRICKY TICKET

I noticed that our entry ticket for the site at Machu Picchu had some unusual writing on the back of it. Another message! Can you read it? A mirror might help you make sense of it.

You are near the end of your journey.

A ruined Inca city on top of a remote mountain has cast a spell since the world learned of its existence 100 years ago. What was it for? Why was it abandoned? We are still discovering the answers.

MACHU PICCHU

THE LAST INCA

Atahualpa was the last "true" emperor of the Inca. He came to power in 1532, after a civil war against his brother. But Atahualpa's reign coincided with the arrival of a band of Spanish explorers. Driven on by stories of a kingdom of gold high in the Andes, Spanish leader Francisco Pizarro led his men and horses to Cusco. Their timing was perfect: the empire was weak at this point in time.

ARRIVAL OF THE SPANIARDS

The Inca Empire fell apart as quickly as it had grown. At the Battle of Cajamarca (left) in 1532, Atahualpa underestimated the Spaniards. With only 167 men, Pizarro easily defeated the Inca and captured the emperor. He promised gold in return for his freedom. The Spaniards took the precious metal but killed Atahualpa anyway.

Golden hands

Hammered designs

MOUNTAIN REFUGE

After Atahualpa's death, the Inca fled to remote cities in the mountains. These cities may have included Machu Picchu ("Old Peak"), high above the Urubamba River. Built by Emperor Pachacuti in the 1400s, the city originally housed only nobles and priests who probably carried out rituals to worship the sun.

TAMING THE SUN

Machu Picchu was a ritual city. Its structures include the semicircular Sun Temple and Intihuatana, the hitching post of the sun. In the winter, when the sun was farthest from Earth, Inca priests "tied" the sun to the stone to prevent it from escaping and make sure it stayed in the sky.

The Inca abandoned Machu Picchu before the Spaniards found it. They headed into the mountains, where the last Inca leader, Túpac Amaru, was captured before being executed in 1572. Over time, vegetation grew over Machu Picchu, and everyone but the local people forgot about it. Then, in 1911, American explorer Hiram Bingham (1875-1956, left) "rediscovered" the ruins— in fact, farmers still lived there. Soon, the whole world knew about the lost city of the Inca.

INTO THE MOUNTAINS

The stall worker led us deep into the mountains. We could see his white shirt ahead of us on the trail. "The Vilcabamba Mountains were the last stronghold of the Inca," said Arturo. "After the Spaniards killed Atahualpa, the Inca lived here in what archaeologists call the lost cities."

We came across people sharing a picnic among some ruins. There was no sign of the stall worker, but Arturo was busy looking at his map. "These walls are definitely Inca," he said excitedly. "But there isn't supposed to be an old settlement here. We must have found one of the lost cities of the Inca!"

Children were digging near a wall. "They're digging for treasure," said Arturo. "People sometimes find Inca objects. Look, one of them has a present for you."

A boy was running toward me. He was holding out something he had just dug out of the ground. He knocked the mud off and revealed . . . a golden corncob! I took my cob out of my pocket and held it next to his. They were identical!

I called to Arturo, who was examining the old walls. "Look," I said. "The boy's corn has a different message on it." Arturo agreed. "And perhaps it will finally explain the message on your corn."

REVEALED!

Arturo said, "This city must have been built by Túpac Amaru. He ruled the Inca after they fled to the mountains to hide from the Spaniards. He was the last Inca ruler of Vilcabamba. For today's descendants of the Inca, he is a great hero who fought for the people's freedom."

SET YOUR CODE WHEEL

This is the last time you'll need to assemble a symbol to learn how to align the arrow on the code wheel. Line up the arrow precisely and hold the wheel in place—otherwise, the clues will not make sense.

What was the connection between my golden corn and the little boy's?

CODE SEVENTEEN: MYSTERY SOLVED

By now, you are probably very used to decoding the messages in the codes. Do not forget, though, that the code contains only the basic words. You may have to change tenses (from the present to the past tense, for example) or guess any missing words.

The little boy was smiling as he listened to Arturo. It was as if he knew a secret. He gave his corncob to me and said something in Quechua, the ancient language of the Inca. I couldn't understand what he said, but some of the people around us began clapping and waving. Arturo knew Quechua, so he translated the boy's words for me: "Welcome home, Julietta, a true descendant of the Inca."

CODE EIGHTEEN: WHO WAS THE MYSTERIOUS STALL WORKER?

On page 48, you will find all of the answers to the Code Quest challenges in this story. Did you get them all right? Good job. Together we have solved the Mystery of the Golden Corn. But what about the stall worker? Did you figure out who he was?

LET'S TAKE A LOOK AT THE CLUES . . .

- He had never appeared at the market in Lima before.
- He dressed like an Indian from the highlands, where the Inca lived.
- He did not try to get his golden corn back; it was as if he wanted me to have it.
- He seemed to be leading us from clue to clue on our journey.
- He led us to a lost city ruled over by the legendary Túpac Amaru.

TÚPAC AMARU

According to today's Inca, Túpac Amaru was a great leader. He helped his people survive for decades after the Spaniards arrived in Peru. In the end, however, he was captured by the Spaniards and executed. That made him an even greater hero to his people.

The Inca believed that their rulers had a close connection to the gods. That meant that they had supernatural powers. Perhaps it was possible that the last emperor continued to watch over his people.

As for the Inca, they are still around. Millions of their descendants still live in Peru, mostly in the Andes Mountains around Cusco. They keep alive ancient traditions such as weaving. Most of the people who live in Lima are descended from the Spaniards. Can you imagine the thrill for one of them to discover that he or she is actually descended from the incredible Inca?

INDEX

AB

Andes Mountains 6, 26, 28
animals 7, 29
Atahualpa (Inca emperor) 40, 41
Bingham, Hiram 41

C

Chan Chan 16
Chimú (people) 16, 35
civilizations, of ancient Peru 16
Coricancha 24
corn 7, 24
crafts 29
crops 7, 33, 35
Cusco (Inca capital) 6, 7, 22, 24, 27, 28, 35, 40, 45

F

festivals 27
food 7, 29

GH

gods 26-27, 28, 32, 35, 45
gold 4, 6, 7, 24, 26, 28-29, 35, 41
hitching posts 27, 30, 38, 41
huacas 35

I

Inca 6-7
empire 29, 35, 41
Inca Trail 25, 30
Inti (sun god) 24, 26, 27, 28

Intihuatana
see hitching posts
Inti Raymi 27
irrigation 7, 34

JL

jaguars 7
jewelry 28, 29
Lima 4, 45
llamas 17, 21, 25

M

Machu Picchu 27, 36, 38-39, 40-41
Mama Kilya (moon goddess) 26, 28
Manco Cápac (Inca emperor) 35
Manco Inca (Inca leader) 34

maps 6, 35
mita (taxes) 29
Moche (people) 17
mummies 16, 17, 18, 27

NO

Nazca 12, 17
Nazca lines 12, 14, 17
Ollantaytambo 34

P

Pachacuti (Inca emperor) 35, 41
Paracas (people) 15, 16
Pisac 32, 34
Pizarro, Francisco 40, 41
potatoes 7
pottery 17, 29

QR

Quechua 33, 45
quipus 7, 20-21, 39
roads 6

S

Sacred Valley 30, 32, 33, 34-35
sacrifices 16, 18, 26-27
Sacsayhuamán 34
silver 28-29, 35
Spaniards, in Peru 24, 28, 40, 41, 44, 45
sun 24, 26, 27, 41
sun gods 24, 26, 27, 28

T

temples 7, 24, 30, 32, 33, 35
terraces 7, 33
textiles 7, 15
timeline 35
Túpac Amaru (Inca leader) 20, 35, 41, 44, 45
Túpac Inca (Inca emperor) 35

UVW

Urubamba River 34, 35
Vilcabamba 35, 39, 42, 44
Viracocha (Inca ruler) 35
walls 7, 25, 35
weaving 7, 28

PICTURE CREDITS

The Publisher would like to thank the following for permission to reproduce their material. Every care has been taken to trace copyright holders. However, if there have been any unintentional omissions or failure to trace copyright holders, we apologize and will, if informed, endeavor to make corrections in any future edition.

(t = top, b = bottom, c = center, l = left, r = right): b
Front and back cover: artwork by Brown Bear Books Ltd.

Pages 4l Corbis: Charles Caratini/Sygma; 4r Thinkstock; 6l Topfoto: The Granger Collection; 6tr iStock; 6br Shutterstock; 7 iStock; 7br Werner Forman: Museum für Volkekunde, Berlin; 7tl Topfoto: The Granger Collection; 8t iStock; 10 Shutterstock; 10–11 iStock; 12 iStock; 14 Shutterstock; 15 Topfoto: Silvio Fiore; 16c Alamy: The Art Archive; 16l Alamy: Mireille Vautier; 16r Shutterstock; 17 Shutterstock; 17c Alamy: Nathan Benn; 18 iStock; 20l Alamy: Stock Connection; 21t Werner Forman: Museum für Volkekunde, Berlin; 21b Shutterstock; 22 iStock; 24 Shutterstock; 25 Shutterstock; 25l Topfoto: The Granger Collection; 26l Shutterstock; 26r Alamy: Deco; 26–27 Shutterstock; 27t Alamy: Mireille Vautier; 27c Getty Images: Michael Latz; 27r Shutterstock; 28c and 28l Topfoto: The Granger Collection; 28r Corbis: Craig Lovell; 29l Topfoto; 29 and 29r Topfoto: The Granger Collection; 30 iStock; 32 Shutterstock; 33l Thinkstock; 33r Corbis: Frederic Soltan; 34 Shutterstock; 34l and 34tr Topfoto: The Granger Collection; 34br Topfoto: Klaus Aarsleff; 35 Shutterstock; 36t iStock; 36b Getty Images: AFP; 38 Shutterstock; 39 Shutterstock; 40l The Art Archive; 40–41 Thinkstock; 41tr Alamy: Stock Connection; 41tl Topfoto: The Granger Collection; 41bl Still Pictures: Michael Sewell/Peter Arnold; 41br Corbis: Bettmann; 42 iStock; 45 Thinkstock; 46–47 Shutterstock

This page reveals the answers to the codes and puzzles throughout the book. It also explains how to set the code wheel, in case any of the settings have you stumped.

THE SOLUTIONS

THE ANSWERS TO THE EIGHTEEN CODES:

• CODE ONE (page 10) The label reads, "It takes two ears to learn the secret of the golden corn."

• CODE TWO (page 10) The ticket reads, "Lima to Nazca" (12 = L; 9 = I; 13 = M; 1 = A; and 14 = N; 1 = A; 26 = Z; 3 = C; 1 = A).

• CODE THREE (page 11) The code-wheel setting is SCROLL. The message on the corn reads, "CORN [is the] GIFT [of the] SUN [and] RAIN."

• CODE FOUR (page 14) The Nazca shapes are (top row) whale; human; monkey; (bottom row) dog; condor; parrot.

• CODE FIVE (page 15) The patterns in the cloth read, "[The] GODS BLESS [us with the] GIFT [of] RAIN."

• CODE SIX (page 20) The quipu shows that Conchita came from "Cusco."

• CODE SEVEN (page 20) The name of the ruler was "Túpac Amaru."

• CODE EIGHT (page 21) The code-wheel setting is BUTTONS. The code on the pottery reads, "[The] INCA CITY [gives this] GIFT [to the] GODS."

• CODE NINE (page 24) The code-wheel setting is VILLAGE. The prayer in the garden reads, "BLESS [the] HOME [of the] LAST INCA."

• CODE TEN (page 25) The code-wheel setting is VILLAGE. The symbols on the llama read, "GO [to the] CITY [of the] SUN [in the] MOUNTAINS."

• CODE ELEVEN (page 25) The message on the wall reads, "THE LLAMA POINTS THE WAY."

• CODE TWELVE (page 32) The code-wheel setting is ENVELOPE. The chalk marks say, "FOLLOW [the] TRAIL [to the] HOME [of the] SUN."

• CODE THIRTEEN (page 33) The worn signpost says, "Look for a message in the city that is sacred to the gods."

• CODE FOURTEEN (page 38) The code-wheel setting is TABLE. The message on the hitching post reads, "STRANGERS [have] ARRIVED [so the] INCA GO [to the] HOME [of the] GODS."

• CODE FIFTEEN (page 39) The name in the quipu is "Vilcabamba."

• CODE SIXTEEN (page 39) The ticket reads, "You are near the end of your journey."

• CODE SEVENTEEN (page 44) The code-wheel setting is FOUR XXXX. The message on the boy's corn reads, "[The] CORN [is the] GIFT [of] TÚPAC AMARU [the] LAST INCA."

• CODE EIGHTEEN (page 45) The stall worker is Túpac Amaru, the last Inca leader, who has come back to help Julietta discover that she is one of the true descendants of the ancient Inca.